**A Landmark Productions
and Abbey Theatre co-production**

Audrey or Sorrow

Written by **Marina Carr**
Directed by **Caitríona McLaughlin**

CREATIVES

CAST *in order of speaking*
Mac **Anna Healy**
Grass **Marie Mullen**
Purley **Nick Dunning**
Audrey **Aisling O'Sullivan**
David **Patrick Martins**
Maria **Zara Devlin**
Father **Howard Teale**
Mother **Aislín McGuckin**

Writer **Marina Carr**
Director **Caitríona McLaughlin**
Set Designer **Jamie Vartan**
Costume Designer **Katie Davenport**
Lighting Designer **Sinéad Wallace**
Sound Designer and Composer
Sinéad Diskin
Movement Director **Sue Mythen**
Associate Director and Vocal
Director **Andrea Ainsworth**
Assistant Director **John King**
Casting Director **Sarah Jones**

COMPANY

FOR LANDMARK PRODUCTIONS
Producer **Anne Clarke**
Associate Producer **Jack Farrell**
Production Manager **Eamonn Fox**
Stage Manager **Brendan Galvin**
Assistant Stage Manager
Ciara Gallagher
Marketing Manager **Sinead McPhillips**
Publicity **Sinead O'Doherty**
Graphic Designer **Gareth Jones**

FOR THE ABBEY THEATRE
Producer **Jen Coppinger**
Company Manager **Danny Erskine**
Abbey Stage Manager **Leanne Vaughey**
Production Manager **Andy Keogh**

Producing Assistant **Aoife McCollum**
Technical Production
Co-ordinator **Justin Murphy**
Head of Costume and
Costume Hire **Donna Geraghty**
Costume Supervisor
Síofra Ni Chiardha
Breakdown Artist **Sandra Gibney**
Head of Costume
Maintenance **Vicky Miller**
Cutter/Maker **Tara Mulvihill**
Costume Supervisor Assistant
Yvonne Kelly
Costume Maker **Denise Assas**
Menswear Tailor **Gillian Carew**
Costume Maker **James Seaver**
Props Supervisor **Eimer Murphy**
Props Assistant **Adam O'Connell**
LX Programmer **Simon Burke**
Chief LX **Dave Carpenter**
Sound Supervisor **Morgan Dunne**
Sound Engineer **Derek Conaghy**
Stage Technicians **Larry Jones, Phil Hughes, Pat Russell, Davy McChrystal, Pat Dillon**
Set Construction
Theatre Production Services
Marketing **Heather Maher, John Tierney**
Publicity **Stephen Moloney**
Social Media **Jack O'Dea**
Publicity Image **Patricio Cassinoni**
Irish Sign Language Interpreter
Caoimhe Coburn Gray
Audio Describer **Mo Harte**
Captioner **Jen Sinnamon**
Artistic Director/Co-Director
Caitríona McLaughlin
Executive Director/Co-Director
Mark O'Brien

A Landmark Productions and Abbey Theatre co-production, Audrey or Sorrow was first performed at the Abbey Theatre, Dublin, on 23 February 2024.

ABOUT LANDMARK PRODUCTIONS

Landmark Productions is one of Ireland's leading theatre producers. It produces wide-ranging, ambitious work in Ireland and shares that work with international audiences.

Led by Anne Clarke since the company's foundation in 2004, its work has received multiple awards and has been seen in leading theatres in London, New York and beyond.

It co-produces regularly with a number of partners, including, most significantly, Galway International Arts Festival and Irish National Opera. Its 30 world premieres - and counting - include new plays by major Irish writers such as Enda Walsh, Mark O'Rowe and Deirdre Kinahan, featuring a roll-call of Ireland's finest actors, directors and designers

Numerous awards include the Judges' Special Award at the Irish Times Irish Theatre Awards, in recognition of 'sustained excellence in programming and for developing imaginative partnerships to bring quality theatre to the Irish and international stage'; and a Special Tribute Award for Anne Clarke, for her work as 'a producer of world-class theatre in the independent sector in Ireland'.

In January 2021 it established Landmark Live, a new online streaming platform which enables it to bring the thrill of live theatre to audiences around the world.

ABOUT THE ABBEY THEATRE

As Ireland's National Theatre, the Abbey Theatre's ambition is to enrich the cultural lives of everyone with a curiosity for and interest in Irish theatre, stories, artists and culture. Courage and imagination are at the heart of our storytelling, while inclusivity, diversity and equality are at the core of our thinking. Led by Co-Directors Caitríona McLaughlin (Artistic Director) and Mark O'Brien (Executive Director), the Abbey Theatre celebrates both the rich canon of Irish dramatic writing and the potential of future generations of Irish theatre artists.

Ireland has a rich history of theatre and playwriting and extraordinary actors, designers and directors. Artists are at the heart of our organisation, with Marina Carr and Conor McPherson as Senior Associate Playwrights and Caroline Byrne as Associate Director.

Our stories teach us what it is to belong, what it is to be excluded and to exclude. Artistically our programme is built on twin impulses, and around two questions: "who we were, and who are we now?" We interrogate our classical canon with an urgency about what makes it speak to this moment. On our stages we find and champion new voices and new ways of seeing; our purpose – to identify combinations of characters we are yet to meet, having conversations we are yet to hear.

abbeytheatre.ie

ABBEY THEATRE SUPPORTERS

PROGRAMME PARTNER

CORPORATE GUARDIANS

Bloomberg

RETAIL PARTNER

ARNOTTS

GOLD AMBASSADORS

HOSPITALITY PARTNER

THE WESTBURY

IT PARTNER

 Qualcom

SILVER AMBASSADOR

interpath

RESTAURANT PARTNERS

PLATINUM PATRONS

The Cielinski Family
Deirdre and Irial Finan
Sheelagh O'Neill
Carmel Naughton

DIRECTORS' CIRCLE PATRONS

Tony Ahearne
Pat and Kate Butler
Janice Flynn
Susan and Denis Tinsley
Elizabeth and Masoud Papp
Kamali in memory of Lloyd
Weinreb R.I.P.
Donal Moore R.I.P.

SILVER PATRONS

Frances Britton
Tommy Gibbons
Andrew Mackey
Eugenie Mackey
Eugene Magee
Gerard and Liv McNaughton
Andrew and Delyth Parkes

Thank you to all the above supporters for your continued support of your national theatre.

Your generosity is key to creating a home for Ireland's theatre makers, players and dreamers in the national theatre. Support experiences like the one you've just seen at the Abbey Theatre today by making a donation to the productions of tomorrow.

Scan the QR code to donate.

Audrey or Sorrow

Marina Carr was brought up in County Offaly. A graduate of University College Dublin, she has written extensively for the theatre. She has taught at Villanova, Princeton, and is currently Associate Professor in the School of English, Dublin City University. Awards include the Susan Smith Blackburn Prize, the Macaulay Fellowship, the E. M. Forster Prize from the American Academy of Arts and Letters, and the Windham Campbell Prize. She lives in Dublin with her husband and four children.

MARINA CARR

Audrey or Sorrow

faber

First published in 2024
by Faber and Faber Limited
The Bindery, 51 Hatton Garden
London, EC1N 8HN

Typeset by Brighton Gray
Printed and bound in the UK by CPI Group (Ltd), Croydon CR0 4YY

Marina Carr is hereby identified as author
of this work in accordance with Section 77 of the
Copyright, Designs and Patents Act 1988

A CIP record for this book
is available from the British Library

ISBN 978-0-571-38972-8

Printed and bound in the UK on FSC® certified paper in line with our continuing
commitment to ethical business practices, sustainability and the environment.
For further information see faber.co.uk/environmental-policy

2 4 6 8 10 9 7 5 3 1

Audrey or Sorrow was first performed at the Abbey Theatre, Dublin, on 23 February 2024, in a Landmark Productions and Abbey Theatre co-production. The cast was as follows:

Mac Anna Healy
Grass Marie Mullen
Purley Nick Dunning
Audrey Aisling O'Sullivan
David Patrick Martins
Maria Zara Devlin
Mother Aislín McGuckin
Father Howard Teale

Director Caitríona McLaughlin
Set Designer Jamie Vartan
Costume Designer Katie Davenport
Lighting Designer Sinéad Wallace
Sound Designer and Composer Sinéad Diskin
Movement Director Sue Mythen
Associate Director and Vocal Director Andrea Ainsworth
Assistant Director John King
Casting Director Sarah Jones

For Dermot, William, Daniel, Rosa and Juliette

Characters

Audrey

Mac

Grass

Purley

Maria

David

Mother

Father

Setting 1

A dining room with a kitchen area off.
A stairs that leads into the dining area.

Setting 2

The dining room of Maria's parents.

Setting 3

The beach.

AUDREY OR SORROW

SCENE ONE

Mac and Grass drinking tea out of a doll's tea set.

Mac Oh yes you did!

Grass I did not! I never ever left you on a log in the middle of the stream.

Mac River.

Grass What river?

Mac You wanted to play with Coldette Maline.

Grass Her? She was a fright.

Mac She was your best friend.

Grass For about five minutes.

Mac You're my only friend.

Grass Now. Yes. But then.

Mac You're getting agitated.

Grass No, we're having tea.

Mac Alright we're having tea.

Grass Is it good?

Mac The whiskey in it is good.

Grass Stop right there!

Mac Is it lapsang?

Grass Lady Grey.

Mac Divine.

Grass Would you like a crumpet?

Mac I'd love a crumpet.

Grass You may go to my fridge.

Mac No it's alright.

Grass You may.

Mac No the fridges are separate.

Grass That has to change.

Mac No. No.

Grass In my fridge there is a crumpet with your name on it.

Mac I'm not hungry.

Grass I'll get it for you.

Mac No wait.

Grass What's wrong?

Mac It reminds me of something.

Grass What?

Mac An orange tree, a woman weeping on a terrace, somewhere hot.

Grass That's a false memory.

Mac No a woman was weeping. Then she flung herself backwards while a man stood there with his arms by his side. He said 'Hmm' in Spanish. Hmm. Or was it Portuguese?

Grass We don't know those places.

Mac Grass we were there.

Grass I've never been on a terrace in my life. Orange trees? You're disgusting.

Mac Not as disgusting as you.

Grass Who leaves the bin in the bathroom full of bloody . . .

Mac Stop!

Grass Parading them. Flaunting them!

Mac I can't help it.

Grass Yes you can! Yes you can! Drink your tea.

Mac I'm drinking it.

Grass How is the bridge?

Mac Oh . . . great.

Grass You won?

Mac I believe I did.

Grass Was that old witch there who cheats all the time?

Mac What witch?

Grass Biddy?

Mac Biddy? Oh Biddy. Yes she helped me win.

Grass Did she smile at you?

Mac God no.

Grass Did she smile at you?

Mac Sort of.

Grass Does she still have teeth?

Mac You know Grass everyone has teeth nowadays.

Grass They don't fall out any more?

Mac No. Never.

Grass Why not?

Mac The tooth fairy.

Grass Oh . . .

Thinks.

Is she real?

Mac I believe she is. Yes.

Grass (*thinks*) I thought the tooth fairy took your teeth away.

Mac That's only in our culture.

Grass But when they fall out?

Mac But they don't . . . any more . . . I read an article about it.

Grass Oh.

Mac Apparently when they fall out they stick them back in . . . with . . . eh . . . Sellotape . . . yes that's what the article said. Draphonopholus the tooth fairy, she's the daughter of the tooth fairy queen and she comes around at night and if your tooth gets loose she hammers it back in with a golden hammer.

Grass Miraculous.

Thinks.

Will she be coming here?

Mac Is your tooth loose?

Grass Yes.

Mac Then she'll come.

Grass Will she ring the doorbell?

Mac Yes.

Grass I'll know what time?

Mac It'll be late . . . the article said.

Grass How late?

Mac Um . . . Midnight.

Grass Is she coming tonight?

Mac How loose is your tooth?

Grass Very.

Mac Maybe we should call her.

Grass You have her number?

Mac I forgot to take it down.

Grass Why?

Mac I didn't know your tooth was loose.

Grass I see.

Mac Are you mad?

Grass No Mac I'm just a little disappointed.

Mac I'm so sorry Grass.

Grass Drink your tea.

Mac Look I'll go and get her number now.

Grass No it's okay. I think my tooth won't fall out tonight. Tell me the Sellotape bit again.

Mac After the golden hammer she applies the Sellotape.

Grass Her own? Or mine? Or yours?

Mac Her own.

Grass Because she's not getting any of my Sellotape.

Mac And mine's used up.

Grass And that's my fault?

Mac God no.

Grass You were insinuating something.

Mac I was insinuating nothing.

Grass Get out of my sight!

Mac Will I wash the cup and saucer?

Grass If you go near the sink!

Mac I was only trying to help. You're burdened Grass. There was a time I was always at the sink.

Grass And you looked at my fridge today.

Mac I didn't.

Grass You did.

Mac What makes you think that?

Grass I don't think it. I have evidence.

Mac Oh.

Grass I caught you.

Mac I was dreaming. I don't remember. It wasn't deliberate.

Grass Which is it?

Mac I didn't mean to look at your fridge.

Grass You wanted a crumpet.

Mac I didn't. I swear I didn't.

Grass All you have to do is ask.

Mac I know.

Grass Am I mean to you?

Mac No. Never.

Grass It was you left me high and dry on the log in the middle of the river.

Mac Stream.

Grass More tea?

Mac No thank you I'm . . . I'm . . .

Grass A mince pie?

Mac It's July.

Grass I made some.

Mac Oh.

Grass What do you say?

Mac I have a date.

Grass Whenever things are going smooth between us you have a date. I should put you in a casket right now.

Mac You're getting out of hand. This is teatime.

Grass You brought up your date.

Mac I'm allowed bring up my date. It's within the rules.

Grass When I got that big job, your face, your face looks exactly like it was then. And your eyes are that slimy serpent green.

Mac You're mixing us up. It was I got the big job.

Grass You liar!

Mac It was you left me on the log. It was you threw all my books into the lake that day.

Grass I'll kill you.

Mac The tooth fairy will come with her golden hammer.

Grass That's a lie! There's no tooth fairy!

Mac I got the job! I was brilliant at it!

Grass Calm down, calm down Mac, it's only teatime.

Mac She's coming. She'll get you.

Puts on a scary voice.

Go to sleep darling. Pollonio and Draphonopholus are coming to hammer out your teeth.

Grass Mac. Please.

Mac Can I look at your fridge?

Grass Yes.

Mac Without accusations? Without remarks being passed every time I walk by it.

Grass Yes.

Mac Can I open it?

Grass You can use the sink. You can turn on the taps.

Mac Even the hot one?

Grass Even the hot one.

Mac Don't you ever ever say you'll kill me again! You hear?

Grass Yes.

Mac I'll kill you.

Grass Kill me please.

Mac There's no tooth fairy.

Grass There is.

Mac There isn't.

Grass Draphonopholus. The article. The pillow. The Sellotape.

Mac Where's the Sellotape?

Grass In my handbag.

Mac Give it to me.

Grass Why?

Mac You don't deserve it.

Grass But I need it.

Mac For what?

Grass My teeth.

Mac You'll have to come up with a better reason than that.

Grass My ears.

Mac Why?

Grass So I don't hear.

Mac What?

Grass The wrong things.

Mac That's right.

Grass I get upset about my eternity.

Mac I don't want to hear about your eternity.

Grass I don't want to hear about your date.

Mac What?

Grass Tell me about your date.

Mac No. I'm telling you nothing about anything ever again.

Lights.

SCENE TWO

Grass is on the phone. The phone looks a bit strange. Is it real?

Grass I have to work . . .

Listens.

But I can't leave her . . .

Listens.

No. No . . . worse.

Listens.

Yes she is . . . she . . .

Listens.

I try to reason with her . . .

Listens.

Upstairs. She's smashing wasps with a fork against the windowsill. She makes a paste out of wasp corpses and then eats it. I think I'm going mad.

Listens.

I'm not . . . I'm not making it up. She's been at it for three days and when I asked her why, she said because she's the tooth fairy.

Listens.

No! You listen for a change! I can't take it any more. Who decided I should be the one has to sacrifice everything?
I went to Cambridge. Did you go to Cambridge? Did any of you go to Cambridge? I went to Cambridge when no one went to Cambridge.

Listens.

I am not isolated. I am not lonely. You think I'm making it up. I'm not overreacting. I'm afraid of her. I'm afraid for her.

Listens.

What time?

Listens.

Call me before you arrive.

Listens.

Yes I'll be here.

Listens.

What do you mean I'm not here?

Listens.

Mac (*from upstairs*) Grass!

Grass I have to go. (*Whispers.*) Do you know what it's like waiting for her to appear down the stairs, her mouth full of dead wasps?

Mac (*from upstairs*) Have you seen my phone?

Grass I'm going. I'm going. Bye, bye, bye, bye bye bye.

Puts phone in her pocket.

Mac Grass!

Grass It's on top of the spare fridge.

Mac (*coming down the stairs*) What's it doing there?

Grass You must have left it there last night.

Mac is dressed in suit, coat, briefcase, goes out, gets her phone, comes back in.

Mac Thanks. I'd be searching for hours.

Grass That's alright. You're welcome.

Mac You're up early.

Grass The sky was blue when I pulled back the curtains.
I scratched my armpit and said, up you get Grass, you're up
already unbeknownst to yourself, meet the beautiful day . . .
you look . . . very . . . professional.

Mac Do I look formidable?

Grass Yes.

Mac Frightening?

Grass You always look frightening.

Mac I need to be frightening today.

Grass A big case?

Mac I'm going to take them down.

Grass That's good Mac. I like when you want to take them
down.

Mac It's called justice, doesn't matter what I like. Have you
seen my glasses?

Grass Your briefcase.

Mac My spare pair?

Grass How long have we lived together Mac?

Mac Don't remind me.

Grass Could we get through one morning without you
asking me where your phone is, where your spare glasses
are? You know your phone is on the spare fridge. You leave
it there to charge every night. And you know your spare
glasses are in the pouch in your spare handbag. Because
that's where you always keep your spare glasses.

Mac Sorry. I was just . . .

Grass Making conversation?

Mac No, I was trying to make you feel necessary.

Grass Necessary?

Mac Needed.

Grass I have a life.

Mac I'm very glad you do.

Grass I'd have a life without you.

Mac Of course you would Grass. What's wrong?

Grass Your breakfast is laid out in the parlour.

Mac I can't eat those monstrous breakfasts.

Grass Gorging on wasps again?

Mac Grass are you okay?

Grass Am I okay? No I'm not okay, I'm worried.

Mac Did you have a bad night?

Grass Is it night now?

Mac Last night it was night.

Grass And tonight will it be night? Or morning?

Mac There's a thing called afternoon as well and there's dusk and twilight and dawn.

Grass I dreamt about the tooth fairy.

Mac I shouldn't have brought it up.

Grass No it's not the tooth fairy. I got over the tooth fairy. It knocked me back for about five minutes in the dark but what really upset me was the light in the hall.

Mac I turned it on.

Grass It was the night for turning it off.

Mac No. You specifically told me to turn it on when
I turned in.

Grass I specifically told you to turn it off when you turned in.

Mac You did not.

Grass I did. It woke me. I'll get over it. I'm getting over it,
just you said we have to be open with each other, not let
things harbour and fester.

Mac I didn't sleep so well either.

Grass What could possibly be worrying you Mac?

Mac You.

Grass Me?

Mac You get like this at the start and before we know
where we are you turn into . . .

Grass Into what?

Mac I'm late.

Grass You're not late. I'm the one who's late. Give me my
coat.

Mac This is my coat.

Grass Come on Mac the game is up for tonight.

Mac No please. Five more minutes. My case. I have to take
them down.

Grass You can take them down tomorrow. I'll take them
down today.

Mac I stayed up half the night writing my speech, going
over all the arguments.

Grass That was me.

Mac No you were having nightmares. I heard you. I left the
light on like you said. I can't please you.

Grass (*taking coat off Mac*) My suit.

Mac Grass you know this is mine. I had it made. I've had it since Cambridge.

Grass takes suit off Mac.

Your shoes?

Grass Don't be silly. They're your shoes. My phone.

Mac Where's my phone?

Grass I told you before if you eat my jam from my fridge you lose your phone.

Mac I didn't eat your jam.

Grass Then who did?

Mac You buy the expensive brand for your fridge.

Grass I buy the expensive brand for your fridge too and I put the extra jam in the spare fridge. You know the rules.

Mac What'll I do all day?

Grass Don't you have your job to go to?

Mac You took all my clothes.

Grass You have loads of costumes.

Mac The wardrobe is locked.

Grass What?

Mac The wardrobe is locked.

Grass When?

Mac There's someone in the house.

Grass No. That's over.

Mac It's not.

Grass That's long over Mac. There's no one in the house.

Mac There's you. There's me.

Grass We don't count. I mean there's no one else in the house.

Mac There is. The wardrobe's locked.

Grass I would never do that on you Mac.

Mac I would never do that on you Grass.

Grass Swear.

Mac I swear.

Grass Okay.

Mac You swear.

Grass I swear.

Mac Okay.

Both look up.

Grass (*whisper*) The best thing Mac is to pretend it's not there.

Mac But the stairs. The stairs.

Grass Never mind the stairs. I'll put the lock on the stairs.

Mac Will you?

Grass I will. Now I've made the bread list. Here. I'll pin it to your bra. See here I've written instructions. Buy bread and milk. And here's the money. How do I look?

Mac Beautiful Grass. You were always the beautiful one.

Grass Nonsense. Goodbye.

Grabs briefcase.

My umbrella.

Gets it.

Oh my phone.

Gets it.

Call me if you . . .

Music. David walks down the stairs carrying a baby's white coffin on his shoulder. Dressed in black. Followed by Maria dressed in black, veil over her face. Grass and Mac watch as they process down the stairs and exit through the room.
   Lights.

SCENE THREE

Mac comes on. Throws herself across the armchair. Sound of front door banging but strange, echoing, as if very far away. Grass enters. Looks around.

Mac Grass I read a magazine in the shop. I got the bread.

Grass My half of the loaf is not beside my fridge.

Mac It's in the spare fridge.

Grass I want nothing you put your hands on in the spare fridge.

Mac Oh. I'll put it in your fridge.

Grass You'll do no such thing.
   What about the magazine?

Mac There was a sentence.

Grass Yes.

Mac Emotionally immature.

Grass *(freezes)* Yes.

Mac It struck me.

Grass It reminded you of someone?

Mac Yes.

Grass Who?

Mac Don't get upset.

Grass I can take your onslaughts.

Mac That one in the shop is emotionally immature.

Grass (*relief*) Dolores?

Mac Is that her name?

Grass The one with the ringworm?

Mac Yeah.

Grass That's Dolores. Dolores is not emotionally immature. She runs a shop. An immaculate shop. Her fridges are spotless. She doesn't eat wasps. She stopped believing in the tooth fairy when she was three.

Mac She picks her ringworm.

Grass I don't want to talk about picking.

Mac You're always cross after work. Did you take them down?

Grass No they took me down.

Mac But you said you'd win.

Grass The planets weren't aligned.

Mac It's not planets. It's court. It's arguments. It's law.

Grass Your performance this morning didn't help.

Mac What performance? I was trying to get to work and you took all my clothes.

Grass It won't happen again Mac. I'll make sure and put on my clothes before I go to bed so you don't put them on by mistake. You're very good to go to the shop and get the bread. I know how hard it is for you to do that. To have to watch Dolores pick her ringworm as she punches the till. I don't like her ringworm either, but you see Mac, out there, is a world and people have shops and ringworm and jobs. And if you want to be safe in here you have to let me get to work and win cases and make the money we need to stock up the fridges with all the food you like and all the nice clothes I buy for you that are in your wardrobe, not my wardrobe.

Mac Will you stop the crazy talk Grass. I've made tea. Can we calm down? Can you calm down? And also I need to go to the bathroom.

Grass Who is stopping you going to the bathroom?

Mac There's someone up there. Someone's back.

Grass No. No.

Mac Listen.

Music. Shadow on the stairs. Purley comes down the stairs in a tuxedo.

Purley Is the spare fridge stocked?

Mac Are you the tooth fairy?

Purley No Mac I'm not the tooth fairy.

Goes off, light of fridge opening, he comes back with a bottle of champagne, shakes it, opens it, fizzes it over Grass and Mac.

How are my girls?

Grass Never better.

Mac Do we know him?

Grass He must be one of the remote family ancestors. I think I'll go and play if you don't mind and Audrey needs a bath.

Purley I know. The smell of her sitting up on your bed reading *Vogue.*

Grass Reading my *Vogue*? I'll kill her!

Roars.

AUDREY!

Runs up the stairs.

Audrey! Audrey!

Mac Audrey is out of hand. I cut their hair off when they back answer me.

Purley When my tractor misbehaves I tear off the brakes. That sorts him out. I gut the incinerator. I kick the living daylights out of the wheels.

Mac The inanimate need to know their place.

Purley The animate too.

Mac Excuse me.

Purley I said, the animate too.

Mac I'm sorry I can't hear you. Is that the patriarchy mumbling again?

Purley It certainly is and you better listen young lady! (*Wags a finger.*)

Mac Speak up patriarchy I can't hear you.

Purley What's the matriarchy blathering about now?

Mac Sorry sorry patriarchy let me try and pop my ears.

Blows out her cheeks.

That's better.

Grass comes down the stairs leading Audrey by the hand.

Grass She's awake at last. It's okay Audrey just come down and apologise.

Audrey For the love of God will ye let me gather myself.

Grass You'll do what you're told.
  (*Pulling Audrey along.*) You'll never guess what I caught her doing?

Mac What?

Grass Leaning on the windowsill looking out the window.

Purley The real window?

Grass Of course the real window.

Mac What did you see Audrey?

Audrey I had my eyes closed. It was an accident.

Grass How many times Audrey have I warned you about the dangers of the real window?

Mac Answer Grass.

Audrey I thought it was one of the pretend windows. I saw nothing.

Purley You didn't see the chains?

Audrey No.

Purley The bones?

Audrey I saw a hip.

Grass Did you hear anything?

Audrey I saw a hand reaching.

Mac Where's the ruler?

Purley Broke. Remember? Last time? You broke it on her.

Grass Then where's the tin foil?

Purley I have the tin foil in my fridge.

Mac You mean the spare fridge.

Purley Mac I'm not getting into arguments about the finer points of the fridges right now.

Grass Bring the tin foil.

Audrey It was a terrible crossing. The worst yet. The violence. The fighting at the horizon. All the ones coming back. There weren't enough boats. I don't need this right now. I got delayed. I had to stab my way up the gangplank. It was pitch black and the ferryman hadn't an eye in his head.

Mac No excuses. Put out your hand.

Purley (*coming on with the tin foil*) There you go. Three new rolls. Special offer.

He gives one to Grass and Mac.

Grass Your hand?

Audrey I'm not putting out my hand.

Purley I liked where I was. I don't want to be here.

Audrey Do you think I do!

Purley Give me that murderous hand!

Audrey I think you broke it.

Purley Girls hold her. Hold her down.

They hold her and lay in to Audrey with the tin foil.

Grass This hurts us more than it hurts you.

Panting, walloping, Audrey fights back, gets the tin foil off Mac, lays in to them, everyone lays into each other. Vicious. Blood everywhere. Screams and swoons. Audrey in pitched battle against the three. She succumbs. They stop exhausted. Music to underscore.

Grass Everyone satisfied?

Purley Can we finish her off?

Grass We sort of need her.

Purley Then we're satisfied. Get up Audrey.

Mac Come on Audrey. Up you get. Good girl.

Purley She's trying. Give her a chance.

Grass Will we help you Audrey?

Mac I hate to see a body down.

Purley Come on Audrey. Welcome back. Here sit on my knee. Where are the lollipops?

Mac hands him the lollipops.

Now Audrey you know what happens next.

Audrey (*leans in to Purley*) I'm sorry. I'm sorry for everything. I'll never leave you again.

Purley Will I kiss you and make it better?

Audrey No.

Purley What?

Audrey Yes kiss me and make it better.

Purley (*kisses Audrey*) And now you have a choice.

Holds out lollipops.

Strawberry or lemon?

Audrey I forget.

Mac Take your time.

Grass There's no rush.

Audrey Strawberry.

Purley Excellent.

Mac I thought we decided on lemon.

Grass No, strawberry.

Purley We said we'd stop if she picked strawberry.

Mac Just because strawberry is your favourite.

Purley That's enough Mac. You go too far.

Mac Kiss me Audrey.

Leans her cheek in. Audrey kisses it.

Say what you have to say.

Audrey I'm so sorry.

Mac Mac.

Audrey Mac.

Mac Go on.

Audrey I'll never ever ever do it again.

Mac Wrong!

Grass Calm down Mac. There's one 'never' Audrey and four 'evers'.

Audrey I'll never ever ever ever ever do it again.

Mac Do what again?

Audrey Anything.

Grass Off you go Audrey. We'll all come up and kiss you goodnight in a while. I'll save my kiss for then.

Audrey goes up the stairs with her lollipop. They watch her.

Purley She's getting big.

Mac Too big.

Grass She'll be in Cambridge before we know it.

Purley How was her maths test?

Mac Straight A.

Grass Mac gave her grinds.

Mac I do what I can. Always found maths easy. Grass was in the remedial class.

Grass I was not.

Mac Oh now.

Purley Art was my ace subject.

Grass Don't get us started on art.

Pause.

I don't think Audrey was sorry enough.

Purley We've brought worse to heel.

Mac I'm very fond of Audrey.

Grass Her legs are good.

Sound of hall door, faint, strange.

They're back.

Enter Maria and David. David stands there. Maria sits at the table. Puts her head in her hands. David watches her. Mac, Grass and Purley watch fascinated.

David What is it Maria?

Maria Nothing. I'm tired.

David You didn't enjoy the film.

Maria Why did you bring me to see that?

David I'm sorry.

Maria I shouldn't have to see that on a Friday night.

David I thought it'd be lighter.

Maria Well . . .

37

David It said family viewing.

Maria We're not a family.

David Then what are we?

Maria We were a family. We're not any more.

David These things take time.

Maria Time? What are you talking about? How can you say that?

David Are we coming back to 'it's all my fault'? Is that what you're warming to?

Maria When have I ever said any of it was your fault?

David It feels like you've said it.

Maria It's all my fault.

David No it isn't.

Maria Yes it is.

David What makes you say that?

Maria Just leave me alone. Goodnight.

Maria goes up the stairs. David watches her. They all watch her.

Mac Drama queen.

Purley No, she's sad. I'll go up and talk to her.

He goes up the stairs.

Grass They never listen.

David goes to the fridge. Gets a glass of white wine. Stands in the room. Drinks. Mac and Grass go over and stand beside him. Touch him gently. Mac rubs his arm. Grass takes his free hand.
Lights.

38

SCENE FOUR

Enter Purley and Mac covered in coal dust. Grass sits at table with abacus counting piles of money.

Grass Just a minute.

Counting with her abacus. This is very difficult for Grass.

Okay. Whew. Who wants to go first?

Mac It's wild out there.

Purley My back is broken.

Grass The cold and wet is good for business.

Mac I hope you fed and changed them while we were out there killing ourselves. Keep the little pets warm.

Grass The little pets are fine. Don't worry about the little pets.

Purley Where's Audrey?

Grass Audrey died while you were out. We had the funeral.

Purley *(calls)* Audrey! Audrey!

Audrey *(off)* I'm in the spare fridge.

Purley What are you doing in there?

Audrey *(off)* I don't know.

Grass I told you she was dead.

Mac You must be hearing voices.

Purley goes off and brings Audrey back.

Purley Is she dead or isn't she?

Grass Have it your way. But I won't have you getting too attached to her. She's dangerous. Go up to bed Audrey. Here take these while you're at it.

Gives her a tray of bottles and nappies.

Audrey I need the keys.

Grass removes a key from a huge coloured key ring.

And the code for the pretend door.

Grass Come here. I'll whisper it.

Mac We know the code Grass. You never change it.

Grass I changed it while you were out delivering the coal.

Purley That's cheating. What if I get restless? What if they cry out? What if they're hungry and you're drunk?

Grass I'm never drunk. Go Audrey. You're alive. Don't push your luck.

Audrey goes up the stairs with the tray and the key.

Grass Okay the reckoning. How many bags of coal?

Purley Five hundred and forty-two.

Grass Why not five hundred and forty-three?

Purley I ran out. It's a cold world out there. Poor things trying to light their little fires.

Grass Never mind them, have you any consideration for us? For the family finances?

Purley You're just vexed because you want to write down the number three. It's your best number. You love the number three.

Grass I do not.

Mac You do.

Purley It's a sort of weakness in you.

Grass (*abacus*) Five hundred and forty-two bags of coal? Not five hundred and forty-threeeeeeeee. How much is that?

Purley (*puts a big piggy bank on the table*) This much.

Grass How much did you charge for a bag of coal today?

Purley Five thousand.

Grass Five thousand by five hundred and forty-two is . . .

She begins counting, fingers, abacus, tongue out.

It's a big one.

Mac Two hundred and seventy-one thousand.

Grass wallops her. Mac falls to the floor.

Grass I'm counting! I'm counting! It's my turn to count!

Mac (*grabs Grass by the hair*) But you can't count! You could never count!

Grass grabs Mac by the hair, both pulling and screaming.

Grass Look at my abacus! I'm counting! I'm counting!

Purley Girls! Girls!

Mac No one uses an abacus any more!

Grass What planet were you brought up on!

Purley Girls let go! Let go!

Grass Tell her to let go first!

Mac She started it! She lets go first!

Grass I can stay like this all night!

Purley Let go together! I'll count! One! Two! Three!

Both fling each other away.

Mac Sow!

Grass Agricultural sow! How much did you say?

Mac Two hundred and seventy-one thousand.

Grass And how many bags of coal did you sell?

Mac I was encouraging him.

Grass So you sold none?

Purley She was a great help holding the horses.

Grass That's no good to me. Encouragement gets us nowhere. We need more than encouragement if this house is to run smoothly. (*To Mac.*) We can't afford your piano lessons this week.

Mac Good.

Grass Or your chocolate. We'll have to eat our chocolate while you watch.

Mac We can share.

Grass Sadly not. I have a board to report to. The chocolate cannot be shared in this town. Sorry Mac.

Mac But I fed the horses. I stood in the cold. I helped load the wagon. I fought off the urchins. I threw rocks at them the size of my head. Actually, now that I think of it I did sell some coal.

Grass How many bags?

Mac Three.

Grass You're provoking me.

Mac Ask Purley.

Grass Well?

Purley (*guilty*) What Grass?

Grass Did Mac or didn't Mac sell three bags of coal?

Purley (*looks from one to the other*) She . . . ah . . . she . . . did . . . yeah.

Grass How many bags?

Purley Three?

Grass Three?

Purley Yeah. Three.

Grass Three Mac?

Mac Three.

Grass Where's the money then?
  Three by five thousand is . . . (*Abacus, fingers, tongue.*)

Mac Fifteen thousand but I sold my coal at a different price.

Grass How much?

Mac Eighty thousand.

Grass A bag?

Mac Yes.

Grass Purley you're underselling.

Purley Oh . . .
  (*Points up the stairs.*) . . . they're back again.

Music. They stand and watch as David comes down the stairs with a white baby's coffin on his shoulder. He is dressed in black. He is followed by Maria dressed in black, veil, black handbag. They stop at the end of the stairs, look at each other. Maria nods to David. Exit both past Mac and Grass and Purley. Audrey watches from the top of the stairs.
  Lights.

SCENE FIVE

Enter Mac, Grass and Purley down the stairs in their communion outfits. White dresses, veils, handbags, prayer books, umbrellas, white shoes, ringlets. A suit on Purley. Communion badges on all.

Mac Your dress is lovely Grass.

Grass How could it be lovely when it's the exact same as yours.

Mac I know I wanted a new dress too.

Purley Family tradition girls. Nothing can be done about it. You wear the old grand-aunts' heirlooms and that's the end of it.

Grass Easy for you to say with your new suit.

Purley I wore the christening blanket same as you. Is it my fault the boys in this house get new suits for their communion? I wish there was an ancient family suit I could wear instead of this rigout.

Mac The material was better in the old days.

Purley Where's the lemonade?

Mac We can't drink lemonade in our outfits. Audrey'll go mad.

Grass Where is Audrey?

Mac Putting on her face.

Purley Then I think we could chance a glass of lemonade if we're quick.

Enter David with pram and suitcase. Enter Maria.

David Sit down. I'll make some tea. Or this calls for a celebration.

*Exits. Maria goes to pram, looks in, pats the pram, goes
up the stairs. David comes on with bottle of champagne
and two glasses.*

I got this in . . .

Looks up the stairs.

Maria.

Maria I'm lying down.

David Will I bring up the baby?

Maria Oh . . . yeah . . . sure.

David lifts baby from pram. Goes up the stairs with her.

Grass Do you know them?

Mac Sure I know them.

Purley I think I recognise them from a conference on
digitalis, or was it Coleridge?

Grass In Cambridge?

Purley Where else Grass?

Audrey's voice from above.

Audrey Did I hear someone mention red lemonade?

The three look at one another. Silence.

That's a very guilty silence.

Purley You answer.

Mac I did the last time.

Grass Not my turn.

Audrey Do I have to come down?

Purley (*pleading*) Audrey.

Mac Please Audrey.

Grass Audrey, they wanted to get out the red lemonade but I said no. I said it would upset Audrey.

Audrey If you get a mark on those outfits.

Purley Audrey we're spotless.

Audrey The state of ye. The state of the bathroom after ye. The state of your beds. The state of the playroom.

Roars. Growls. The three shudder. Panic.

Will I come down?

Mac No please.

A giant foot on the stairs.

Purley Audrey for the love of God don't.

Grass Go back. Go back.

Foot hovers, twirls.

Audrey If I have to come down.

Mac Audrey don't, don't, please, we're so sorry, we'd never dream of . . .

Grass We'd never . . .

Purley Not in a million years Audrey. Please don't come down.

Foot retreats.

Audrey Practise taking the host until I finish my face.

Purley Where's the chalice?

Mac In the spare fridge.

Grass I have the hosts here.

Takes them out of her handbag. Purley runs and gets the chalice.

Purley Put them in.

Grass does.

Line up girls.

Mac and Grass, hands joined, line up.

Mac first.

Mac closes her eyes tight and puts her tongue out.

Purley Your tongue's out too far.

Mac Audrey said to stick it out as far as I could.

Purley Relax. Stop dribbling.

Grass I'll show you. Watch me Mac.

Grass closes eyes tight, sticks out tongue.

See it's easy.

Purley Body of Christ.

Grass (*with tongue out*) Amen.

Mac Aren't you meant to put your tongue out after the amen bit?

Purley Mac's right. Here let me show you. I'm a bit of an expert on this.

Gives her chalice.

Grass The body of Christ.

Purley Amen.

Sticks out his tongue, Grass puts host on his tongue, Purley blesses himself.

David (*from above*) Okay bye darling.

Mumble from Maria.

You have everything?

Mumble.

Will you rest with the baby or will you get up?

Mumble.

I'll make the dinner when I get home.

Mumble.

It's fine. The fridge is stocked. I did the shopping before
I collected you.

Mumble from Maria.

I don't mind. I'm just happy it all worked out . . . this time.

*Mumble from Maria. David walks down the stairs. Mac,
Grass and Purley watch him. David gets his briefcase.
Stops. Goes to bottom of the stairs. Looks up. Hold.
David exits.*

Purley He shouldn't leave her on her own like that.

Mac He has a briefcase. He has to go to work.

Grass It's a very important case. He has to bring them all
down.

Purley I know, but still.

*Baby wails. Maria runs down the stairs, walks through
Mac, Grass and Purley, sits at the table. Baby wails
throughout.*

Grass Should we go up?

Mac To the baby?

Purley Better not to interfere.

Grass Audrey will take care of it.

Mac She won't.

Grass Poor little thing.

Purley (*goes to Maria, whispers*) Go up to your baby Mam.

Maria looks around.

Grass (*whispers*) Your baby is sad.

Mac (*whispers*) Your baby is choking.

Maria goes up the stairs. The baby calms. Maria sings 'Hail Queen of Heaven' from above. Mac, Grass and Purley listen.

Grass That was close.

Mac Well done for speaking up.

Purley We all spoke up.

Grass The baby is okay.

Lights.

SCENE SIX

Mac, Grass and Purley watch as Maria sets the table for two. David brings on two plates of dinner. They sit.

David (*blessing himself*) Bless us oh Lord and these thy gifts which of thy bounty we are about to receive through Christ our Lord amen.

Maria looks at him. He pours wine for them. They eat and drink in silence.

Is it okay?

Maria David you know you're a better cook than me.

David On some things.

Maria I'm not hungry.

David Did you eat anything today?

Maria I think so.

David If you don't eat we'll have to take you to the doctor.

Maria He'll just tell me to eat.

David Maria, what's wrong?

Maria Can you just stop.

David Is it Purley?

Maria What do you mean is it Purley?

David You still blame yourself.

Maria Wouldn't you?

David Maria, these things happen.

Maria But it happened to us David. It happened to us.

David I know it happened to us.

Maria I don't know how you can sit there and say your grace before meals. Bless us oh Lord for these thy gifts. What gifts? We're not blessed. We're cursed.

David How can you say that? We have each other. We have a beautiful baby daughter asleep upstairs in her cot.

Maria I'm afraid.

David What are you afraid of?

Maria That what happened to Purley will happen again.

David It won't.

Maria How do you know?

David I just know.

Maria Well I just know it will.

David Don't say that.

Maria Maybe it has happened already.

David (*looks at her*) What are you saying?

Looks up the stairs.

Maria This house is haunted.

David That's nonsense.

Maria I hear whispers, noises, the fridge door keeps opening.

David It's an old fridge. It opens on me sometimes too.

Maria I smelt something.

David What did you smell?

Maria I smelt someone near the baby.

David When?

Maria Lots of times . . . just before I came down.

David jumps up. Runs upstairs. Maria sits there. David comes down.

David She's perfect. She's sleeping. I felt her heart rise and fall. She's breathing. Peaceful.

Maria It's Purley.

David Purley died two years ago Maria.

Maria But he's here. He's still here. He didn't want to die David. He didn't want to. He wants to be near us. He wants to be near me. He hates the new baby. He thinks it should be him in the cot. I think so too. I don't like this new baby. I want Purley back. I didn't want this baby. I wanted Purley back. Why wouldn't you listen to me? I told you. I want Purley. I don't want this baby.

David Darling that's not a well thing to say. She's a baby. It's not her fault Purley died.

Maria He's not dead. And if you must know I think it is her fault. I think she wanted to be born and she never would have unless Purley died. So now what are we going to do?

David She. Her. The baby. Why won't you call her by her name?

Maria You only name things you love. You only name things you want. If you don't name a thing, it's not really here is it?

David Maria, I'm so sorry about Purley. I'm so sorry I wasn't even here.

Maria I don't blame you for that. You were working. One of us has to work.

David But you went through it on your own.

Maria I should have held him while he slept. I should never have put him in his cot for his nap. I should have watched his every breath. How can you watch every breath? And when I go out I hear the whispering, the looks, there's always doubt over a cot death. Did she do something? In a moment of madness did she do something to her baby? You wonder too.

David I don't. I swear I don't. I didn't. I never did.

Looks at her.

Maria . . . did you do something to Purley?

Maria You see. That's what I mean.

David You wouldn't. You'd never.

Maria You see. Now the doubt is there. It was there all the time.

David It wasn't. You have me afraid now.

Maria I did nothing to Purley. I went to lift him from his cot after his nap and he wasn't breathing. He was alone for an hour. He was sleeping on his back the way they tell you.

The right way for a baby to sleep in his cot. I picked him up. He was cold. I sat on the bed with him. Sometimes they breathe so softly, so quietly, you think they're dead. I held him. I thought, he'll take a breath in a second. But he didn't. I swear that's what happened.

David I believe you. I've always believed you.

Maria Do you?

David Yes.

Maria Do you really?

David I said yes.

Maria Because I don't. I know I didn't do anything I shouldn't have but someone did.

Looks around.

Someone or something in this house did.

David What makes you say that?

Maria Because someone brushed by me on the stairs as I went up to lift Purley from his nap.

David What brushed by you?

Maria It was a woman.

David What woman?

Maria I don't know. A woman.

David Did you see her?

Maria No I didn't see her but she was there. She's still here.

David What?

Maria She's upstairs somewhere.

David Is she upstairs now?

Maria Yes.

David And you leave the baby up there?

Maria Where else am I to put the baby?

David (*gets up*) I'm going up to her. The baby.

Maria No don't.

David Why?

Maria Sometimes I look in the cot and the baby is gone.

David That can't be.

Maria She takes the baby sometimes.

David Takes the baby where?

Maria She takes the baby and then she puts the baby back. I'm afraid someday she'll take the baby and won't return her.

David goes up the stairs as Audrey comes down the stairs. Maria sits there.

David (*from upstairs*) Maria. The baby's here.

Maria Well that's good then. Isn't it?

Lights.

SCENE SEVEN

Audrey stands watching Mac, Grass and Purley come down the stairs with books.

Audrey Sit down.

Mac, Grass and Purley sit down.

Today I'm going to teach you about the wind. Ready?

All three nod.

Now I could rattle on for hours about all the different kinds of winds in the world. The trade winds, the west wind, the

54

east wind, the arctic wind, the local wind, the periodic wind, the celestial wind, the wind from the moon and the wind from Mars, the eternal wind, the first wind, the wind of Time, but you're not sailors and any fool can look up their winds. No, what I want to tell you is the most important thing about wind. The wind rises, the wind blows and then the wind dies. Like all the people in the fields, in the cities and towns, every last mother-born one of them, urban and rural, don't be fooled when they act like they're alive. They are wind and like the wind, they rise, they blow and then they die. We know better don't we?

All Three Yes Audrey.

Purley As the poet says, more than one life looks through our eyes.

Audrey What poet?

Purley Em . . . I don't know. Lines come in my mind from nowhere or from other times. Are you cross with me now Audrey?

Audrey No Purley. I forget sometimes that you're an old old soul, like me. Now, who's alive?

All Three You are Audrey.

Audrey That's right. Who else is alive?

All Three We are.

Audrey Correct. And who's dead? Hands up?

All three put their hands up.

Mac.

Mac Everyone except us.

Audrey Everyone except us.

Grass But Audrey.

Audrey Yes Grass.

Grass Maria and David.

Audrey What about them?

Grass They don't seem dead.

Audrey Ghosts often act like they're living. They get a bit mixed up.

Purley You mean they don't know they're dead?

Audrey No they forget or no one ever told them.

Mac But Audrey, Maria has a new baby.

Audrey It's not real.

Grass But we heard it crying.

Audrey That was me.

Grass That was you?

Audrey You don't believe me?

Mac But the baby crying. It was so real.

Audrey Did it sound like this?

> *Does a heartbroken new born baby wail? Maria enters on the stairs in her nightdress.*

Maria Purley? Purley I'm here darling, where are you?

David (*entering on stairs in pyjamas*) What is it? What?

Maria Did you hear it?

David What's wrong?

Maria Purley is crying.

David Purley?

Maria He wants me. He wants us. He's frightened.

David There's nothing Maria. You dreamt it, or the wind, or a cat.

Maria There's someone down there.

David turns on the light. Audrey, Mac, Grass and Purley all look up.

David Look there's no one.

Purley wails this time. He starts walking up the stairs towards Maria.

Maria There. Purley. I can't believe you don't hear him.

David There's no one. There's not a sound. Come back to bed.

Maria But he might be suffering.

David He's dead Maria. He was baptised. He's in heaven. He's at rest.

He leads Maria back up the stairs.
    Lights.

SCENE EIGHT

Maria sits at the table breastfeeding the baby.

Maria (*strokes the baby's head*) You've enough?

Wraps baby in blanket and puts her in the pram. Goes out. Mac and Grass come down the stairs.

Mac You slept well.

Grass I did Mac, and you?

Mac I always wake at three.

Grass At three? That's nice of you Mac, to say three so nicely.

They look into the pram.

Mac A beautiful baby.

Grass She looks like you.

Mac Like me?

Grass Yeah. You were a beautiful baby Mac.

Mac Do you remember me as a baby?

Grass Oh yes.

Mac But I'm older than you.

Grass None of that matters. I remember you.

Mac In your pretend memory?

Grass No in my real memory. You see I looked down. I was waiting to be born and I couldn't be until you'd grown up a bit.

Maria enters with a bar of chocolate. Checks the baby. Sits at the table and eats the bar of chocolate. Mac and Grass watch her.

Post-natal depression.

Mac What's that?

Grass When you have a baby it makes you sad.

Mac Oh. Why?

Grass Because it dawns on you that you've brought something mortal into the world and it has to die.

Mac That's terrible.

Grass It is.

Mac I'm never having a baby.

Grass I might.

Mac How?

Grass Purley knows what to do.

Mac What do you have to do?

Grass It's like doing a really hard big girl jigsaw.

Mac Go on?

Grass When you've a bit more sense Mac. You don't need to know any of that yet.

Mac Does it involve a bed?

Grass It does.

Mac Does Audrey have to be there?

Grass Definitely.

They look up.

Mac I love Audrey.

Grass I love Audrey too.

Mac And Purley.

Grass What would we do without Purley.

Mac And I'm getting to like Maria.

Grass Don't get too fond of her.

Mac Why not?

Grass She's dead.

Mac But she's kind. She loves the baby. It's so lovely to watch. When I can't sleep I go in to watch her with the baby. I get into the cot sometimes and lie beside the baby. And when Maria looks at the baby or smiles I sometimes think she's smiling at me. I keep really quiet.

Grass Does Audrey know?

Mac Don't tell Audrey.

Audrey (*from above*) Don't tell Audrey what?

Mac and Grass freeze.

Don't tell Audrey what?

Audrey comes down the stairs.

Grass Mac gets into the cot with the ghost baby.

Audrey Oh that's allowed.

Mac Are you happy today Audrey?

Audrey (*looks into the pram*) I am.

Goes to table. Blows on Maria's hair. Maria turns.

Go upstairs girls. I need to say a few words to Maria.

Mac I thought we weren't to talk to Maria and David.

Audrey Mac do as you're told.

Grass Come on Mac. I'll keep an eye on her Audrey.

Audrey Thank you Grass.

Grass Audrey . . . you won't do anything to the baby.

Audrey Of course not.

Grass It's just . . .

Audrey What?

Grass I saw . . . I'd hate that to happen again.

Audrey That was an accident.

Grass I know but . . .

Audrey I wept bitterly over that.

Grass I know Audrey.

Audrey I fell.

Grass I know but . . .

Audrey But what?

Grass Maybe I saw wrong.

Audrey You did Grass. You saw very wrong. I slipped in the dark. That's all there is to it.

Grass I know . . . but Audrey?

Audrey Yes Grass.

Grass You can see in the dark . . . we all can.

Audrey Grass when you're older you'll understand. Maria needs help. She needs quiet. Look at her. All she does is eat chocolate and weep.

Mac But that's normal when you have a baby.

Audrey What would you know about what's normal?

Mac I read an article about it . . . in *Vogue*.

Audrey Who gave you permission to read *Vogue*?

Mac It was lying there. David buys it for Maria. I didn't know it's forbidden.

Audrey Grass take her upstairs. Teach her the 'Hail Queen of Heaven', she doesn't know it properly.

Mac It's too glorious. I get confused with the beauty of the Queen.

Audrey That's enough Mac. Where's Purley?

Grass The pub.

Audrey Okay leave me. Leave us.

Mac and Grass go up the stairs holding hands. Maria eats chocolate. Audrey goes to the table. Sits opposite her. Looks at her.

Audrey You're thinking of the old place aren't you? The house by the sea. I think of it often too.

Maria looks at the pram.

The pram. The pier. The rest of it.

Maria puts her hand over her face. Music.

It's alright Maria. It was a long time ago. The great times we had. Great times altogether. The light on the waves. The starlings on the shoreline digging for worms. Thousands of them. We had the baby in the pram. We chased the starlings into the sea. They flew and flew. Into the waves. We took off our shoes and socks, tucked our dresses into our knickers and ran into the waves after them. The cold Atlantic. Then we dried our feet with our socks and then put on our wet socks. You helped me fasten the buckles on my shoes. You fixed my dress. We ran to the pram and then we went home and Mum made us toast with bananas and jam and we had some Pak orange even though it wasn't Sunday.

Pause.

A beautiful day Maria. Remember that. You were also good to me. Remember that.

Maria sighs. A long broken sound.

You were very good to me until you weren't. I don't forget that. I love you. I look up to you. I would never harm you or anyone belonging to you. Talk to me. Tell me what's wrong. Go on. Tell me. Tell me please. Maybe I can help you.

Maria goes to the pram.

Maria (*to the baby in the pram*) Not David. Not Purley. Not you. Nothing makes sense. I look at you and you look like a cat or a bear. I think I'm breastfeeding a bear, with your claws and your brown fur.

Audrey stands beside Maria, both looking into the pram.

Look at you. Sleeping the sleep of the dead, smelling of my sweat and my milk. Poor baby. Poor baby bear sucking on my milk that smells of clay and mackerel. And you look like my dead sister. You look like Audrey.

Audrey No, the next one will look like me. This one is the image of you Maria. Purley looked like me too, the black hair, the white skin, the cornflower eyes. This one looks like you Maria. This one is ugly. I'm tempted to leave you this one just so you can look at the image of yourself every day of your life. To look and remember. To look as in a mirror. Isn't that what children are for Maria? To look and look and remember.

Maria (*not to Audrey, to the air*) Audrey forgive me. Forgive me. Forgive me, forgive me. I didn't mean it. I didn't really. I didn't. It was an accident. Wasn't it.

Audrey (*to Maria*) Of course it was Maria. I know it was. Just as Purley was an accident. Just as this one will be an accident.

Maria No!

Picks baby up.

No one, no one will harm you. You're not the baby I want but no one will harm you. No one. I want Purley.

Weeps.

I want Purley.

Audrey And Purley wants you.

Does a baby cry, a haunting wail from far away?

Maria (*looks around helplessly*) Stop. Oh Stop. Purley stop. I can't come to you.

Audrey You could swap them.

Does baby wail again?

Maria Purley. Purley.

Holds out a hand as if to catch him, baby in the other arm. Audrey does baby wail.

Where are you?

63

Enter David.

Audrey cries, baby wails, very faintly. Maria stands there demented holding the baby, arm outstretched.

David What's wrong?

Maria You hear it too?

David Is she hungry?

He goes to the baby. Audrey's crying stops.

She's asleep.

Maria David.

David Maria what is it?

Maria She's not breathing.

David What?

Takes the baby.

Maria I just fed her. She was sleeping. I was afraid. I just lifted her.

David Christ. Oh Christ. Christ. What have you done Maria?

(*To baby.*) Breathe. Breathe. She's gone. She's cold. What have you done?

Audrey stands there looking at them. David stands with the baby. Maria stands with her mouth open. Mac comes tearing down the stairs very upset.

Mac Audrey, Audrey I had a terrible dream. I was in my mother's arms and I died. I was in a blue blanket. It was in a room like . . .

Looks at David and Maria and baby.

Audrey I told you to stay upstairs.

Mac What did you do?

Audrey Me?

Mac What did you do to the baby?

Audrey I tried to stop it. They're ghosts Mac. They don't matter. Leave them be.

Mac That's her isn't it? That's my mother.

Audrey You can't tell Grass.

Mac Why can't I tell Grass?

Audrey It'll upset her.

Mac Grass isn't born yet?

Audrey That's right.

Mac To these ghost people?

Audrey That's right Mac.

Mac But if they're ghosts what are we?

Audrey We're the living.

Mac How are we the living?

Audrey Death doesn't last very long Mac. Look at you. Look at me. Look at the wonderful lives we have.

Mac Did you ever die?

Audrey Many times.

Mac Tell me.

Audrey It's boring. It was all so long ago. I'm weary of it. Look at them, so sad, so full of themselves with sorrow.

Mac What does it mean Audrey?

Audrey Mean? It doesn't mean anything. Over like that. (*Clicks her fingers.*) Did you learn your 'Hail Queen of Heaven'?

Mac I have it now.

Audrey Good.

Mac But the baby. Maria. Look at David. Look at their faces.

Audrey It's called fate Mac.

Mac Will they lose Grass too?

Audrey No, poor Grass will survive.

Mac But that's not fair.

Audrey I know Mac but we have to leave them with something.

Mac But me and Purley, it's not fair on us.

Audrey It wasn't fair on me either. Do you know what your mother did to me?

Mac Maria?

Audrey Yes Maria. Do you know what she did to me?

Mac No.

Audrey Will I tell you?

Mac Was it horrible?

Audrey Beyond horrible.

Mac Then I don't think I want to know Audrey, unless Grass knows.

Audrey Grass doesn't know.

Mac Grass is your favourite child.

Audrey Yes she is.

Mac Was I ever anyone's favourite?

Audrey Never.

Mac That's what I thought. But I kind of hoped. Were you?

Audrey Oh yes Mac I was the favourite. The great favourite. That was the problem.

Mac Can I look at the baby before we go up to do the 'Hail Queen of Heaven'?

Audrey Go on then.

Mac goes to baby in David's arms.

Mac That's me isn't it?

Audrey It is.

Mac Which of them killed me?

Audrey Maria.

Mac How did she do it?

Audrey By wishing it.

Mac I couldn't resist her.

Mac pats baby's head.

Audrey No, you're weak Mac. You don't have the grey matter, the charm, the resolve.

Mac Do I not?

Audrey But it's not your fault. Not many can withstand the kind of hate Maria gives off.

Mac Oh. I always thought she was a gentle sort of creature.

Audrey So did I Mac. Lovely even.

Puts out her hand. Mac takes it. They go up the stairs. Maria and David look at each other.
  Lights.

SCENE NINE

Purley and Grass on the floor, drawing, cutting out and colouring up a storm.

Purley Grass is this a right cathedral?

Grass Show?

Examines the picture.

It's not too bad but you need a spire with a cross on it.

Purley I want Audrey to be happy about this picture. She said my cathedrals were coming on great altogether.

Grass Where's Mac? She should be drawing her orchids. Her orchids are terrible. She has to improve soon or Audrey will be cross with her.

Purley Audrey's always cross these days.

Grass Since Maria and David moved in.

Purley I wish they'd leave.

Enter David down the stairs with a child's white coffin on his shoulder. He is dressed in black. Maria follows him dressed in black. David stops at the bottom of the stairs. Maria pauses halfway down.

David Are we ready?

Maria Yeah.

David Please try and control yourself this time.

Maria I will David. I will.

David Would you rather stay here? Let me take care of . . . it?

Maria No I'm coming.

David You won't jump in the grave?

Maria Will Purley's coffin be visible?

David I expect it will Maria. It's the same plot.

Maria I can't face your mother.

David My mother is devastated.

Maria She blames me.

David No she doesn't.

Maria And your father . . . I know the way he'll look at me. I can hear him thinking, baby killer, baby killer.

David Maria this is crazy. I was here. I know it had nothing to do with you. It's just one of those terrible things.

Maria And Purley? Was he just one of those terrible things?

David Yes, he was.

Maria Two terrible things.

David They're all lined up outside. I don't think you should come.

Maria I have to come.

David Then please, please, compose yourself.

Maria I am. I am. I will.

David Okay. Are you ready?

Maria puts her veil over her face, nods.

Maria But I can't speak.

David I'll do the speaking.

And they exit, stately, with the coffin. Echoing sound of the door closing. Music.

Purley They're going to the cathedral.

Grass (*colouring*) Yeah to bury the baby. It's called a funeral.

Purley I know. I remember my own.

Grass Do you?

Purley It was in a cathedral too. They put me in a white box like the one David was holding.

Grass I can't wait for my funeral. Was it nice in the box?

Purley It was middlin' nice and Audrey got up on the altar beside your man. She said the mass.

Grass Was it night?

Purley They like to bury babies at night.

Grass I wonder why?

Purley Everyone's embarrassed and it's unkind to make people look one another in the eye. Better moon, star, shadow, the confessional blocking out the light, let the mother weep into her veil unhindered, let no one speak of the muck and the worm.

Grass Do you remember the worms?

Purley I do. And the claws. And you turn into, you know that awful porridge Audrey makes?

Grass Yeah?

Purley I put my hand to my face and it was porridge. My nose floated away, teeth and fur in my eye. Something was sucking on my eye.

Grass I remember the worms.

Purley But you couldn't.

Grass Why couldn't I?

Purley You're talking through your hat. You're not here Grass and you're not there. Give me a break.

Enter Audrey down the stairs, dressed in black, prayer book, veil, followed by Mac dressed to the nines in a little girl party dress, in white, flowers in her hair, rosary beads dangling, prayer book. Mac sings 'Hail Queen of Heaven', or music to accompany.

Off gallivanting I see.

Audrey Maria and David need a bit of support.

Mac We're going with them. We're following the hearse. Audrey made me a new dress. We're following my coffin.

Grass Whose coffin?

Mac The baby.

Grass You said 'my' coffin.

Audrey You know Mac can't get her thoughts in order. Her sentences don't come out properly. She's weak on the possessive.

Grass Do you like my picture Audrey?

Audrey It looks familiar.

Grass It's starlings on the beach and that's you and that's . . .

Audrey Maria.

Grass I wish Maria could see it.

Audrey (*tears it in two*) Too much imagination Grass. I told you to draw coal.

Grass I'm sick of drawing coal. Why must I always draw coal?

Audrey Because someday you will be coal Grass. Someday we'll all be coal. Coal is a beautiful thing. Look if you need a break from coal. Draw rocks.

Purley Your dress is lovely Mac.

Mac Why do I feel I'm swallowing clay?

71

Audrey Let's go Mac.

Purley Can we come?

Audrey No, I need you to stay here and mind the house. Maria and David will be sad when they get back.

Purley But they ignore us.

Audrey No they don't. That's just the way of ghosts. They know we're here.

Grass I kissed Maria the other day. She was sitting on the stairs crying and I kissed her cheek and I swear she put her hand to her cheek and said, whoever you are, thank you.

Purley I kiss her every night at three.

Audrey Poor Maria. Life can be terrible, terrible, relentless, even when the sky is blue and you wish you were . . . oh never mind. Come on Mac.

Exit Audrey and Mac. Purley and Grass colour for a minute.

Grass Purley.

Purley Hmm?

Grass I think Audrey killed the baby.

Purley Yeah she killed me too. Twice.

Grass What?

Purley She loved me so much she wants me to live forever so she killed me. It didn't hurt, well not that much, all the air went and that was a bit scary but only for a minute and then she took me in her arms and here I am.

Grass Oh.

Purley When I was a ghost my name was . . . um . . . it'll come to me. A long time ago. What's this my name was at all?

Grass Did Audrey kill me too?

Purley No she's going to leave you with the ghosts.

Grass I don't want to be left with the ghosts.

Purley Do you want me to kill you when you're a ghost?

Grass God yes. I don't want to be stuck in a pram with Maria.

Purley Audrey can be a bit cruel sometimes.

Grass What has she done now?

Purley Well . . . Mac. Audrey's bringing Mac to her own funeral.

Grass Is that not the done thing?

Purley No it's not the done thing.

Grass But Audrey said that Mac needs to toughen up a bit.

Purley Mac is Mac. I think it'll make her weaker. Of all of us I think Mac would've made the best ghost. She's so empty. She's the most like David and Maria don't you think? That slow way they have. Ghosts. So closed off in themselves like tombs.

Grass Mac would make a great ghost. Is Mac the baby that Audrey just killed?

Purley Of course she is.

Grass Why?

Purley Why did Audrey kill her? I don't know. She doesn't love Mac the way she loves me.

Grass Or me.

Purley Mac's the black sheep definitely. I'm not sure but I think Maria and Audrey had a fight.

Grass When?

Purley Maria stole Audrey's doll or knocked down her sandcastle on the beach. Never draw a beach Grass. Audrey hates them. Yeah I think that was it. Maria stepped on Audrey's sandcastle one day and I think there was a shell involved. Audrey has never forgiven it.

Grass Audrey doesn't forgive.

Purley No.

Grass Is it good to forgive?

Purley Audrey thinks so.

Grass But she can't do it.

Purley I think it was a big sandcastle that Maria knocked.

Lights.

SCENE TEN

Maria walks in, dressed in black. She looks around, looks up the stairs. David comes in, goes back out, comes in with whiskey and two tumblers.

David Do you want one?

Maria No.

David It'll help.

Maria I don't care.

He pours one for himself, drinks. Maria stands there, hands hanging. He pours her one. Puts glass in her hand. She looks at it. He drinks. Silence.

David Maria.

Maria What?

David We're still here.

Maria Are we?

David We are darling. We are. Look . . .

Maria stares at him.

Maria My mother didn't come.

David She never comes.

Maria My father didn't come.

David Your father. Maria, they didn't come to your wedding. They didn't come to the christenings. They sent nothing. When they were born, not a flower, not a card, not a phone call. Why did you expect them to come?

Maria Death is different.

David It certainly is.

Maria Your mother weeping, clinging on to you.

David She was very upset.

Maria You tell me to compose myself but your mother can wail and scream and have to be held back by your father and by you. I nearly clocked her one. You'd swear it was her baby going down into the muck. And Purley's coffin, it's rotten already. I saw a foot.

David You did not.

Maria I saw an infant foot, scraped clean. I saw rat teeth on the bones of an infant foot.

David You did not.

Maria And you know what else I saw? I saw Audrey.

David Audrey? . . . Your sister?

Maria Do we know another Audrey? As we walked away from the grave, I saw Audrey.

David You couldn't have seen Audrey.

Maria I saw her approach. Audrey. But Audrey grown. For a minute I thought it was my mother, my mother had come. But no, it was Audrey. She had a spade. She was digging up my baby's grave. She's come to take her the way she took Purley.

David Maria, you couldn't have seen that.

Maria I know but I did. She was singing.

David Yes there was singing. The choir was there.

Maria No, Audrey was singing.

David Audrey died when she was five.

Maria Seven.

David Five. Seven. What does it matter. Audrey died when she was seven.

Maria I never told you how Audrey died.

David A drowning wasn't it?

Maria That's right.

David A rogue wave.

Maria A rogue wave . . . we were on the pier. This wave out of nowhere. We were playing with the pram. Audrey was strapped in it. I was the mother. She was the baby. And this wave . . . and I let go . . . we were warned never to go to the bottom of the pier where it's all sea and sky but we went. The pram floated. I could see her struggling with the straps but I'd knotted them because the pram was old and the straps were broken. I had her tied in very tight. We were running down the pier and I let go. It's a slope. I wanted to give her a thrill. There was no rogue wave. That's what they said after for . . . decorum. There was no rogue wave. I flung her into the sea. I was five. That's when I became the stranger in the family. The ghost . . . You should leave me. It's clear I can't do this.

David I can't leave you. You're expecting.

Maria I'll get rid of it.

David You'll do no such thing.

Maria Do you believe in evil David?

David Why do you ask me that?

Maria You should. I'm evil. I'm proof there's evil in the world.

David You were five.

Maria I knew what I was doing. For years I pretended I didn't. Now I know the truth. I knew what I was doing. And the strange thing, the strangest thing of all?

David What?

Maria I adored her. I adored Audrey.

David (*goes to her, wraps himself around her*) Maria, I'm so sorry about Audrey. I'm so sorry what happened to you. You were so young for a thing like that to happen.

Maria My mother couldn't look at me. When I came into a room my father would leave, not in any aggressive way, he just couldn't be in the same room as me for very long. He'd sort of pat the air above my head and leave, couldn't touch me, I gave him the shivers. It was the way the ropes were tied in the pram. Audrey wanted them that way. We were playing prisoners. It was the way I tied the ropes and the flour bag knotted around her neck. I said, can you breathe Audrey? She said, yes, she could breathe fine . . . When they found her, the sea, the rocks, all that, but the ropes were still knotted, her hands still tied behind her back, the flour bag still on her head fastened at the neck.

David A pretty terrible game.

Maria I think so now. I thought so then.

David Why did you let go?

Maria (*looks at him*) Because I'm the type of person who lets go if given the chance.

David Did you kill Purley?

Maria I knew.

David What? You knew what?

Maria I knew you thought I did.

David I didn't.

Maria But you think it now?

David Did you?

Maria No.

David And the baby we just buried? The baby you wouldn't name?

Maria Audrey was here.

David Forget about Audrey. Did you kill her?

Maria I don't think I did.

David You don't think you did? It's very simple. Did you or didn't you?

Maria I wanted Purley.

David So you did?

Maria No. No. All I know is I wanted Purley back. And I picked her up and she was gone.

Enter Audrey covered in muck followed by Mac covered in muck from head to toe. Mac is sobbing.

Audrey (*leading her up the stairs*) It's alright Mac, I'll wash it all off.

Mac But my . . . my . . . my . . . my . . . oh . . . oh it's . . . there's a stone in my throat . . .

Audrey That's normal . . . ssh . . . ssh . . . I'll make crumpets if you stop crying.

And they're gone. Echoing sound of a door opening and closing.

Maria Audrey . . . said if I swapped . . . but that's all, David. I think that's all.

Lights.

SCENE ELEVEN

Dinner table in Mother and Father's home. Sound of the sea. Night. A huge sky of stars visible.

David So they say anyway.

Handing plate to Mother.

That was amazing.

Father We eat straight from the sea here.

Mother Maria, maybe you'll get the port. Cheese for anyone?

Father I'll have some of the Gortnamona love and the Gubbeen and that big smelly Brie whatever you call it.

Mother David?

David Why not?

Mother (*passing the pram*) Ah look at her.

Maria Is she awake?

Mother Staring at her hands. I used love that when you were small, the way they lift their hands and turn them over as if to say, what on earth are these supposed to be for?

Leaning into the pram.

Anyone could do anything to you. Wouldn't stand a chance.

Grace. Little Grace. Great name. Aren't you taking your life in your hands calling a child of yours that. When you phoned to say you were coming. With Grace. Your father looked it up.

Exit Mother.

Maria Dad, you'll have a drop of port.

Father It means favour. Gift. Divine bounty bestowed on us. Unearned. An unearned blessing.

David Well isn't she?

Father Pardon. It also means pardoned.

Looks at her.

Thank you Maria.

Mother enters with cheese.

Mother Do you feel pardoned Maria?

Maria Never.

Mother Do you David?

David Do I what?

Mother Have you pardoned Maria?

Father Are you favoured?

David By whom?

Maria Some port?

Mother Leave it there dear. I like to pour my own. Someone must have eaten the Brie. Maria?

Maria I don't really like cheese.

Father Audrey was the one for cheese. And smoked salmon. I'd sit her on my lap and she'd eat a side of salmon if she was let. Maria never liked eating.

Mother Unless it was ice cream or chocolate.

David She's still the same.

Father Still a sweet tooth Maria?

Maria Well I suppose . . . I won't starve.

Father But really if you had a fligget of imagination or self-preservation you wouldn't have called this child Grace.

Picks up baby from the pram. Holds her aloft.

Do you know what Grace really means? To call a child Grace is asking for its opposite. Divine wrath. Divine anger. Boiling Divine anger. Divine tragedy. Divine sorrow.

Maria It is not.

Mother Ignore him.

Father And sorrow now. There's an interesting word. From the Middle English. *Sorwe.* Your mother knows all about *sorwe.* All three kinds of *sorwe.* There's personal sorwe. There's external sorwe. And then there's supernatural *sorwe.* Important to know which kind it is you feel because *sorwe* does not make you great or stronger or wiser. It depletes. It ravages. It devours until you can't remember there was ever a thing called joy. Ask your mother there drowning in her three kinds of *sorwe.* And which kind will you dispense, little Grace, in your blanket? Because from here you look like a great sorrower come to our feast. You come like a great sorrower, like a ghost, bled out.

Kisses the baby.

David Give her to me.

Father What? What's wrong?

Maria Give her to him.

Father Nervous Nellies.

Holds the baby. Looks at them. Hold. Hands over the baby.

There she is. You think I'm going to bounce her on her head. I've held enough of them.

Caresses the baby's leg.

But have they earned you Grace?
   Your pardon?
   Don't they owe a debt? Haven't they fallen from Grace? Were you ever deserving of Grace?

Mother I will kill you in your sleep if you don't stop. I swear, I'll clock you with this cheeseboard!

Father Enough with the histrionics.

Mother Waffles . . . That's what I was thinking about earlier. The summer all you and Audrey wanted to eat were waffles. They were new. You'd got them at someone's house and all the pair of you wanted was waffles.

Maria I don't remember an obsession with waffles.

Mother What do you remember Maria?

Maria It's good of you to have us . . . to visit . . . the baby . . .

Father The baby's lovely. She's breathing isn't she? All that matters. Duty discharged. Keep them breathing.

Mother Don't mind him. We're old and battered. Leave the young folk my love. Let them realise for themselves the disaster it all is. Time will leave her claw marks on them too. In your heart did you think we were dead?

Father We wrote. We called. We turned up on your doorstep.

David When?

Maria You did not.

Father You sent the letters back. Hung up every time.

Mother Slammed the door in our faces.

Maria I did no such thing. How could I have when you weren't there? I was the one who wrote, who called.

Mother I threw those letters in the sea. Into the sea with Audrey. Let her read them. Pathetic.

Father Can we dispense with the lies and deception?

David As you know Maria has had a . . .

Mother We know.

Father You're here now and welcome you are.

Mother We'd love you to stay as long as you want. This is your home Maria.

Maria Yeah.

Father You are ours.

Mother Always.

Maria I'm so sorry.

Mother About what?

Father What's to be sorry about?

Maria No listen, I'm so sorry about . . . about . . .

Mother Audrey?

Maria No . . . well yes . . . that too . . . but I was going to say something else.

Mother Oh I thought you were finally going to apologise about Audrey.

Maria No . . . yes . . . but . . .

Father What are you trying to say Maria?

Maria I don't know . . . I . . .

Mother That it should have been you?

Maria Maybe.

Father Nonsense. Don't ever say that Maria. Ever. Why should it have been you?

Mother No dear, it wasn't you. It was Audrey. Stupid girl, you could tell her nothing. She had our hearts scalded.

Maria Really?

Mother If she could do the opposite of what you told her, she'd do it. Isn't that right love?

Father Let's not speak ill of the dead. It was a long time ago. She was only a child.

Mother A tormented one. She had you bossed out of existence. The tantrums about her hair, her dolls, her shoes, her throat, eating coal. Do you remember love, the winter she sucked on coal?

Father I suppose I do love.

Mother And school? She ripped the face off poor Miss Skelly because Miss Skelly had put an X beside her page of Rs, all written backwards. Nearly took her eye out. I see Miss Skelly still, still has the scar under her eye. I look at her and think, here you are still carrying my daughter's scar and my daughter is dead. Audrey. Robbing all the other children's lunches, flushing them down the toilet, had me disgraced.

Father But then the devil would leave her and she'd sit on your knee and fall asleep.

Mother The baby has a great look of her.

Maria Does she?

Mother When you walked in the door with the baby, Audrey, I said Audrey has come back to us. You were a good child. We never blamed you for Audrey.

Maria Did you not? . . . Do you not?

Father What could put that in your mind?

Maria Well . . .

Mother Never. You were five for God's sake. She was a demon. I blame myself. I shouldn't have let you off that day but she had me demented and Purley had a temperature and was squalling the house down.

(*To Father.*) You were gone as usual. So I bundled ye into your coats and wellies and off ye went with the old pram full of dolls. And I warned Audrey. I warned her. And she promised me. If I said it once I said it ten times. The pier. The pier. Promise me Audrey you'll mind Maria and promise me you won't go near the pier. And she did, butter wouldn't melt. I should've known but I was distracted, waiting for the doctor to come and see Purley and the pair of you had the house torn down. I thought, I'll go mad. I will go stark raving mad. So I flung ye out the door and said don't let me clap eyes on ye till teatime . . . and what with all that happened at the pier and Purley gone a few days later. You know what that is Maria. I lost two. You lost two. We know what that is. Neck to neck. Even. Quits on loss anyway. Stalemate.

Maria Is that what it is?

David Purley? You're not talking about our Purley are you?

Father Do you own the name Purley?

David I never knew there was another child. Called Purley.

Mother Patrick but we called him Purley.

David Maria you never told me.

Father Did you not?

Maria I don't remember any Purley . . . except my own. Was he the stillborn one?

85

Father He was born just fine. Perfect.

Maria Oh . . .

Father He lived for six months . . . he was allowed live for six months.

David Allowed?

Father Yes, allowed.

David What do you mean? Who allowed him?

Father Now that's the great question. Who allowed Purley live for six months?

Mother The ones who decide allowed him.

David And who are they?

Mother Do you think for one second you're in charge?

David Of my own allotted portion? Yes I do.

Mother On this tiny rock, a thousand byways and billions of light years from the centre of the Milky Way, a by-lane off another by-lane, we reside. An abandoned cliff edge, behind a mountain of dead stars and exhausted moons and burnt-out suns, miraculously we reside and flourish. Do you honestly think any of this could happen without someone somewhere at some time deciding it must be so?

David But what happened to Purley? Meningitis?

Mother Cot death.

David Cot death.

Mother (*to Father*) You found him love.

Father So you say.

Mother I do say.

David Oh . . . I found . . .

Father Then you know what's involved.

Pause.

Can we talk about something else love? What were we talking about?

Mother Forgiveness. We were talking about Audrey. You see I was so demented over Audrey I forgot about Purley. I mean I did all the things you're meant to do with a baby but on automatic. He had a sort of fever but he was getting better. He was on antibiotics and I gave them to him and he was improving. He seemed chirpier but what did I know. All I could think was Audrey, Audrey, Audrey. I couldn't believe it. And while I was mad with grief somehow I let Purley slip away.

Father Leave it love. It's over. All done and gone.

Mother And I suppose I forgot about you too dear. Did I?

Maria No . . . no . . . no . . .

Mother I did. I did. I'm sorry Maria. I'm sorry dear.

Maria Can I ask you both something?

Father What is it?

Mother What? You have me frightened now.

Maria It doesn't matter.

Father Ask. What is it Maria?

Mother Tell us. Is something wrong again?

Maria I wouldn't be here if something was wrong.

Mother Then what?

Maria Have you felt anything?

Mother Felt what?

Father Felt anything?

Maria Audrey.

Mother looks around.

Father Audrey? What are you saying?

Maria Just . . . that . . . have you seen her?

Mother You mean . . .

Father Never. Never. None of that nonsense. Never. We've never seen her Maria.

Mother Have you?

David Maria.

Maria No . . . not exactly but I've felt . . .

Father Ah felt! Felt! They die Maria. They don't come back.

Maria Unless they do. Unless we do. Keep on and keep on coming back.

Mother I have felt her.

Father Now love.

Mother No! You listen. I have felt her on the stairs, she eats the cheese, she knocks over my wine, she bites, she pushes, she stomps around the house.

Maria Have you seen her?

Pause.

Mother Yes I've seen her. Have you?

Maria No.

Mother Has she spoken to you?

Maria I don't know . . . No . . . I think so.

Mother You think so. I know so. And you know what she told me Maria?

Maria What?

Mother That Purley wasn't a cot death.

Maria Your Purley?

Mother Yours my dear.

David This is . . .

Maria He was. He was.

Mother Or the second one wasn't a cot death. The one you didn't baptise.

Father Or our Purley wasn't a cot death.

Mother Our Purley was a cot death. I have the doctor's certificate. I have the inquest report.

Maria I have . . .

Father You have only my trust!

Mother Your trust?

Father Yes my trust! My belief! My blind eye!

Mother Your blind eye? You're unbelievable! You were the one who found him! God knows what you could've done!

Father Who lets two children play on that pier in the middle of winter? At high tide? I know things love.

Maria You saw her Dad?

Father looks at her.

You spoke to her?

Pause.

She spoke to you? She took Purley? She took the two of them?

Mother The three of them.

Father That's the story around here. Blame Audrey. Blame my little Audrey.

Baby cries in the pram. All look at the pram. No one moves.

David She might stop if we're all quiet.

Father She's having a bad dream.

David They cry a lot.

Father Heartache.

David I'll just take her up and nurse her a bit.

Mother Leave her.

David stops.

Let her cry. Let her get used to it. Never getting a damn thing you want and stop looking so smug with your new child in your new pram. When I think of what you've actually done.

The baby cries through the rest of the scene. Building and building to a heart-rending wail.

Maria What have I actually done?

Mother And now this . . . this . . . poor innocent creature . . . at your mercy.

Father I'll tell you what you've done, the pair of you, I'll tell you if no one else will. You've brought her into death. You young people so cocksure of yourselves with your perfect new baby. You'd think she was the only child ever born.

David What? I'm sorry what? Don't speak to Maria like this. Your daughter.

Mother My daughter.

Father That's all it is. The minute they're born. That's on your heads. When you lie down with a fertile woman, a fertile woman like a field, you sow death in the world.

Death in the form of black-haired, brown-haired, golden-haired children. Well, we stole one from the grave. One out of three. You. Maria. Not bad odds. Not great odds but not bad either and I suppose you've managed to do the same. You can thank me for that.

Mother Your vigilance is it?

Father Yes my vigilance. My vigilant eye my love.

Mother His vigilant eye kept you safe.

Maria Safe from what?

Father And if you're wise young man you'll keep a vigilant eye in your head too.

Maria I said safe from what? Safe from who?

Mother From me he means. You know Audrey was born dead and . . .

Father They don't need to hear this!

Mother It's true. She was born cold as a stone. No heartbeat. Never drew breath they said. You were there. You saw it. And they wrapped her in a blanket and brought her to me to say goodbye and I took the blanket off her and pulled my nightdress up and laid her tiny cold body against my skin and they kept trying to take her off me and I beat them away and held her naked dead body against my naked heart. And it could have been hours, could have been minutes, time stopped or reversed or whirled around us and I prayed to God and the Virgin and every saint I know to give her back . . . I howled the hospital down and they're trying to wrestle her off me and sedate me but I fight them off and hold her fast and . . . she starts to get warm and the marble blue of her skin turns grey and then white and then begins to blush and then her heart beats against mine, a drum in a forest far away, a tiny echo, stopping and starting, stopping and starting until she finds her rhythm and her breath comes as real as mine . . . I brought her back . . . I brought her back . . . every doctor and nurse in the hospital converging to see the miracle . . . the old tea lady with her trolley weeping and wringing her hands . . . all of us weeping and laughing, even you.

Father Even me.

Mother I brought her back . . . I brought her back.

Father When maybe you should have submitted . . . and let her go. The insatiable need and greed of mothers but who can blame you for being the way that Nature made you?

Mother You understand absolutely nothing.

Father Don't I?

Mother Must be marvellous to be so secure in your delusions.

Father Magnificent. Pass the port. Did I hear you saying you're going on the beach tomorrow?

Maria I thought I'd show it to David.

Father There are other beaches to show David.

Maria I want to show him that one. I want to walk on the pier. That's all.

Mother You doubt her? Even still you doubt her?

Father I'll watch from the window.

Mother I won't be watching.

Maria What's to watch. David swimming. Me and the baby sunning ourselves. The forecast is good for tomorrow. Waves. Sky. Horizon. Starlings. Home.

Lights.

SCENE TWELVE

The beach. Blue sky. Sound of the waves. Breeze. Cries of birds. Salt light.

Maria and David come across the beach. Maria wheels the pram. David carries the bags.

David Here?

Maria Here's fine.

Looks in pram.

David How is she?

Maria Asleep.

David (*laying out towels*) You going to brave the cold Atlantic?

Maria Maybe. Are you?

David In a bit.

Baby sounds from the pram. David looks in the pram.

The sea air wake you?

Takes baby out of the pram.

Look at you. Smiling. Maria she's smiling.

Maria She does that a lot. Don't you Gracey Grass?

David Why do you call her Grass?

Maria Don't know. She reminds me of grass, so fresh, the smell of her, so bright.

David (*to baby*) If I say so myself you're the best looking baby I've ever come across. You are. Yes you are. I think she might be hungry.

Passes her to Maria. Maria puts her on her breast.

I'm hungry myself.

Maria I made sandwiches and there's a flask of tea.

David (*stripping off*) A swim first. I think I'll swim over to the pier. Will you be okay here?

Maria Of course.

David You sure?

Maria Stop fussing David. I'm fine.

David You are, aren't you?

Maria Grass is nearly one.

David The danger is passed.

Maria If you can get them to one.

David That's what my mother says too. Get them to one and they'll generally make it.

Maria Nearly there.

David Your mother and father. I'm glad you've sorted it out with them.

Maria Liars.

David What do you mean?

Maria All that hogwash about Audrey.

David They seem a bit unhinged.

Maria A bit? They're ghouls . . . Never mind. Let's not think about them. After our swim we're driving home Purley I mean David. Home with Gracey Grass and we're never coming back here again.

David And Rome next week. We'll hold her up to be blessed. We'll have a good summer Maria.

Maria Lots to look forward to.

David This is the beach?

Maria Yeah.

David That's the pier?

Maria Yeah.

David You're okay about it?

Maria About what?

David Being here.

Maria It's perfect. I had good times here too.

David Your parents are fond of Grass at least.

Maria Who doesn't love a baby?
(*To baby.*) And such a baby. You know David, maybe this is a terrible thing to say but I've forgotten the others. I've forgotten Purley and I never thought I would. I never think of him now and if I do it doesn't upset me.

David Time.

Maria And the other little one. I never give her a thought at all. Do you?

David Sometimes . . . I do . . . yes . . . I often think of them.

Maria In a way they were trial runs. Grass is our first.
(*To baby.*) Aren't you Grass? Our first and only.

Baby gurgles.
    Pause.

David You call for them sometimes.

Maria Do I? . . . No . . . When?

David When you're asleep.

Maria I'm not responsible for the night. What are you the sleep police?

David I'm just saying, you call them.

Maria I do not. Or if I do I don't remember. I wake clear headed. I reach for Grass. Don't I Grass? And you smile at me. And your eyes. Your ancient blue eyes.

David I didn't mean to upset you.

Maria You didn't. It's okay David. Relax, trust me. I'm happy. Your daughter is beautiful, the sun is bursting out of the sky, the waves are coming across the golden sand. The starlings . . . the starlings . . . have your swim. Look at that horizon. Blue on blue. I'm no good on colours but that's a blue you'd hope to see when you're washed up on the shore of the next world.

David Madonna blue.

Maria Is that what it's called?

David I think so.

Kisses her, kisses the baby.

These last months . . .

Maria I'm glad if I can make you happy David.

David Are you happy?

Maria Can't you tell?

David I think I can.

Maria That nightmare is gone. Gone.

David I'll wave from the sea.

Maria Don't go too far out.

David Don't be silly.

Maria Still, never trust the sea.

David I'll keep to the shore.

Pats the baby's head.

Hold her up when I'm out there. See if I can make you out.

He runs into the sea. Maria watches him. Waves. Laughs.
Holds the baby up. Puts the baby in the pram. Rocks it
for a while. Hums 'Hail Queen of Heaven'.
  Enter Audrey. Sunglasses. Red lipstick, scarf in her
hair, holding her sandals, looks at Maria, looks out.

Audrey Ah . . . the starlings . . . still here . . . isn't that
something. The waves . . . the sky . . . the pier.

Maria takes off her blouse, rolls up her skirt, lies down
on towel, sunbathes. Audrey goes to the pram.

Grass (*from the pram*) Audrey.

Audrey Ah Grass. How are you getting on?

Grass How long will I be stuck in this thing?

Audrey Go back to sleep.

Grass When do I get to walk?

Audrey Don't be so spoilt. You don't know how lucky you
are.

Grass But nothing works. My tongue, my hands, my legs
are so wobbly, Maria talks down to me all the time, David
wakes me up to make sure I'm breathing. I'm having a nice
snooze, the only thing to do with the boredom of it, and
next thing a poke in the ribs, the mirror clapped up to my
nose, if there's steam on it I'm breathing.

Audrey I've watched. They're good to you, they parade you
everywhere. You met my mother.

Grass Who?

Audrey Granny?

Grass Oh her. Is she your mother?

Audrey Did you like her?

Grass No and the auld fella, the grandad, he's your father
then?

Audrey He makes the best pictures.

Grass How long will I be dead?

Audrey Go to sleep.

Grass I miss Purley and Mac.

Audrey You miss Mac? No one misses Mac.

Grass Where are they?

Audrey Purley? Who knows. Mac got on a bus.

Grass She's gone pinching. Mac has an awful pinch. She was great at making all the dead scream on the highways and byways. When can I come home Audrey?

Audrey You want to come back to us? Go to sleep Grass, you look ridiculous.

Audrey looks at Maria. Sits beside her. Looks out. Maria raises her hand. Waves. Audrey copies her.

Maria.

Maria sits up. Looks around. Jumps up.

Maria What? . . . Who are you?

Audrey Hello Maria.

Maria goes to pram, looks in, puts her hand on the pram.

Maria I'm sorry do I know you?

Audrey Have I changed that much?

Maria I think you're mixing me up with someone else.

Audrey Not a bit of me. Beautiful day. The starlings. The pier. Many days like this one. Two sisters. A pram.

Maria No . . . You? . . . Audrey? . . . No.

Audrey A bit arrogant don't you think to come here and play happy families.

Maria I'm not . . . I've been thinking about you all day . . . thought if I came here you might . . . you might . . . Did I do it on purpose?

Audrey I've pondered that question myself.

Maria Mum thinks I did. She still thinks it.

Audrey I watched you through the window last night. She was smiling. You were laughing. Your eyes were shining.

Maria That was for show . . . because of David . . . because of the baby. She took out all the old photographs . . . album after album of you.

Audrey Don't try to sweet-talk me.

Maria I'm not. She has loads of you in your coffin, a black album. She keeps it on the table beside her bed.

Audrey And Dad?

Maria This morning I was in the kitchen, very early, couldn't sleep, making tea and he appears in the doorway. He jumped when he saw me, like I was a ghost, backed himself out into the hallway clutching his heart. I visited your grave. I brought flowers. I left a letter.

Audrey Flowers. Letters. Graves. You'll never find us there.

Maria Do you walk? Much?

Audrey I do.

Maria Are there many of you?

Audrey More than of you. Purley's here.

Maria Purley's there?

Audrey And Mac is here.

Maria Who's Mac?

Audrey Your second one.

Maria Oh is she? . . . No heaven then?

Audrey (*looks around*) Oh I wouldn't say that.

Gets up.

You want to chase the starlings?

Maria looks at her.

Drive them into the sea?

Maria I don't think so.

Audrey A walk on the pier then?

Maria I have the baby.

Audrey We'll bring the baby.

Hand on the pram.

Maria No.

Audrey Would I harm your baby?

Maria I don't know.

Audrey Your sister? Would you harm me?

Maria Never.

Audrey Then let's go.

Wheeling the pram off.

Maria I'll come. Leave the baby.

Audrey You sure?

Maria Yes. Leave the baby.

Audrey Up to you.

*And exit both. Pram left on stage. Hold. Pram rolls
slowly towards the sea.
Lights.
End.*